Original title:
Hypothetical Hearts

Copyright © 2024 Creative Arts Management OÜ
All rights reserved.

Author: Giselle Montgomery
ISBN HARDBACK: 978-9916-90-654-5
ISBN PAPERBACK: 978-9916-90-655-2

Entrapments of a Life Divided

Two roads diverge beneath the trees,
One whispers softly, the other, a tease.
I stand in the shadows, torn and confused,
By choices I made, by paths I have used.

A heart split in fragments, each beat feels strained,
The laughter of yesterday now feels unclaimed.
Echoes of moments dance in my mind,
Yet shadows of doubt leave me feeling blind.

With dreams like a puzzle, pieces misplaced,
Sifting through memories, time has erased.
Each turn of the page offers pain and delight,
A tapestry woven in day and in night.

I gather the threads of what could have been,
A life stitched in fragments, a dance on the wind.
Yet here in this chaos, I search for a sign,
To mend all the pieces, to blend them in line.

The Game of Ghosted Hearts

In shadows dance the unsaid things,
Whispers lost on unseen wings.
We play the game, a silent part,
Chasing echoes of the heart.

Each glance a spark, each sigh a flame,
Yet words dissolve, and none to blame.
We linger close, yet drift apart,
In this game of ghosted hearts.

Illusions of a Distant Embrace

Across the void, a flickering light,
A promise held in waning night.
In dreams we meet, in whispers we sigh,
Yet come the dawn, we're worlds awry.

A phantom touch, a fleeting taste,
In every moment, time lay waste.
We reach for warmth, yet find cold space,
In illusions of a distant embrace.

A Symphony of Untouched Echoes

Silent notes in the air do play,
Tales of love that slipped away.
In shadows cast, the music strays,
A symphony of untouched days.

Resonance lingers, soft as a sigh,
In empty rooms where memories lie.
Each echo dances, yet we stay blind,
To the symphony we've left behind.

The Mystery of Incomplete Stories

Pages turn but words remain,
Fragments left in the rain.
What once was whole, now torn apart,
The mystery of an incomplete heart.

In every glance, in every pause,
Unraveled plots, we search for cause.
Yet in the gaps, new tales ignite,
In the mystery of our silent fight.

Petals in a Wind of Whimsy

In gardens bright where colors bloom,
Petals dance, dispelling gloom.
They twirl and spin on gentle breeze,
A soft embrace through rustling leaves.

Whispers carried from flower to sky,
As dreams awaken, they soar high.
Each fragrant note, a fleeting song,
In this moment, where we belong.

Chasing Shadows in the Dawn

When golden rays creep through the night,
Shadows retreat from morning light.
Chasing dreams that flicker and fade,
In the hush where hopes are laid.

Footsteps echo on dewy grass,
As time slips by, like moments pass.
With every beat, the heart takes flight,
In the dance of day and night.

Pictures Framed by Unseen Hands

In corners rare, the silence hums,
With whispers soft, the memory comes.
Each frame reveals a hidden tale,
In shadowed light, where dreams prevail.

Captured smiles in faded hues,
The laughter shared, the tender views.
Unseen hands craft the perfect scene,
In spaces where we once have been.

The Realm of Perfectly Untouched Moments

There lies a place where time stands still,
Moments untouched, a heart to fill.
With every breath, the world slows down,
In quiet magic, where dreams are found.

The canvas waits for colors bright,
A heartbeat's whisper, pure delight.
In this realm, we're free to roam,
In perfectly untouched moments, we find home.

Heartstrings in the Ether

In the whisper of the night,
Hearts dance like distant stars,
Silent threads of light entwine,
Echoes of who we are.

Beneath the canopy above,
Dreams drift on velvet skies,
Each heartbeat a gentle push,
Towards unseen, sweet replies.

Moments weave a tapestry,
Of laughter, sighs, and tears,
In shadows and in sunlight,
We conquer all our fears.

With every breath we take,
Our spirits intertwine,
In this endless realm of hope,
Our destinies align.

Enchanted Possibilities

A forest filled with wonder,
Where dreams begin to grow,
Each path holds a secret,
Barefoot, we wander slow.

The air hums with enchantment,
Colors dance with delight,
Possibilities are endless,
In the fading light.

Whispers of the ancients,
Call out from the trees,
Guiding us through twilight,
On a gentle breeze.

With every step we take,
New worlds unfold in sight,
Together, hand in hand,
We claim our right to flight.

Chimeras of Connection

In the mirror of your eyes,
A universe takes shape,
Fragments of a shared story,
In dreams, we escape.

Threads of fate intertwining,
In this intricate design,
Chimeras come to life,
In moments so divine.

Each word a feathered whisper,
That dances in the air,
Unseen bonds between us,
No distance can compare.

Together we are stronger,
In the silence, we find grace,
Chasing after echoes,
Of love's warm embrace.

Uncharted Emotions

On a canvas of our hearts,
Colors swirl and blend,
With each stroke of emotion,
New horizons extend.

Navigating the unknown,
With courage as our guide,
Through valleys deep and wide,
We turn the tide with pride.

Every tear that we've shed,
Transforms into a spark,
Illuminating shadows,
Lighting up the dark.

Together we explore,
This vast terrain of soul,
Charting uncharted waters,
With love as our control.

Unreality's Caress

In shadows dance the fleeting dreams,
Where whispers weave through silent streams.
A world where reason takes its leave,
And heartbeats pulse in threads we weave.

Beneath the glow of moonlit haze,
Imagination's vibrant maze.
Each thought a brush, each sigh a stroke,
In colors of the heart bespoke.

Reality fades, a gentle tease,
As fantasies embrace the breeze.
With every glance, a new horizon,
In realms where hope is ever risin'.

So let us drift in this embrace,
In unreality's soft grace.
For in those moments, pure and bright,
We find our truth within the night.

The Art of What-If

A canvas spread of endless dreams,
Where possibilities burst at the seams.
What if the stars could hear our plea?
What if our hearts could truly see?

In every choice a path unfolds,
The stories that the brave have told.
What if the past could be rewritten?
What if the pain left us smitten?

With colors bold, we paint our fate,
In shadows dark, we contemplate.
What if the dreams we dare to chase,
Lead us to love in a kinder place?

So ponder well this art divine,
In each small thought, a world to find.
What if tomorrow brings us peace?
What if our longing finds release?

Unfathomable Yearnings

In the depths where silence calls,
Rest hidden hopes beneath the falls.
With hands outstretched, we seek the grace,
Of love that time cannot erase.

Yearnings deep as oceans wide,
Where secrets of the soul abide.
A yearning heart that knows no bounds,
In endless echoes, longing sounds.

In every sigh, a storm begins,
As dreams collide with hidden sins.
The ache of wanting, fierce and clear,
With every heartbeat, drawing near.

Yet still we chase the distant light,
Through darkest hours of endless night.
For in the shadows, hope still sways,
Unfathomable through endless days.

Echoes of Truths Untold

In whispers soft, the stories fade,
Echoes linger in the glade.
Truths once spoken gather dust,
In hearts that learn to love and trust.

Each secret hides a world within,
Where honesty and shadows spin.
In silent vows we find our place,
As memories etch on time's face.

The truths we fear are yet untamed,
In murmurs soft, their voices named.
As night befalls and stars ignite,
We seek the light beyond the fright.

So let us share the tales we keep,
In echoes deep, our hearts won't sleep.
For in the sharing, bonds unfold,
Revealing echoes of truths untold.

The Unfolding of Forgotten Dreams

In shadows cast by years of night,
The whispers of lost hopes take flight.
Beneath the stars, they softly gleam,
A testament of what might have been.

Through tangled paths of memory's maze,
The heart remembers brighter days.
With every sigh an echo lost,
A haunting tune of dreams at cost.

Like paper boats on rivers wide,
They drift alone, the dreams we hide.
Yet in the stillness, hope remains,
A flickering flame that softly gains.

If dawn could break this silent bind,
The echoes fade, and dreams unwind.
In morning light, the past takes form,
Creating futures from the storm.

Hardships of Not Quite Together

In corners dark, we tread our way,
On paths that twist and oft betray.
With every step, the weight we bear,
A silent cry, a muted prayer.

For hands are clasped yet hearts divide,
In shadows cast, we try to hide.
The laughter fades, replaced by sighs,
In fractured bonds and longing eyes.

Each moment stretches, time stands still,
We chase the warmth, yet feel the chill.
In fleeting touch, the dreams cascade,
Like autumn leaves in twilight fade.

Yet through the storm, we stand as one,
In every battle fought and won.
For even torn, our spirits rise,
To find the light that never dies.

The Nostalgia of Unmet Signature

Within these pages, ink remains,
A story lost, yet still retains.
In every line, a vision clear,
A pen that trembles, hope and fear.

As faded letters softly glow,
The tales we weave, the seeds we sow.
Yet signatures lie, unfulfilled,
In whispered dreams that night has stilled.

Echoes linger, memories drift,
Of paths untaken, chance, a gift.
With every choice, the silence clings,
To fleeting moments that joy brings.

But in the heart, a spark resides,
Of what could be, where love abides.
And so we write with fervent hope,
For every dream, a new day's scope.

The Ballad of Untethered Dreams

Upon the hills where shadows play,
A melody of dreams in sway.
With every note, the heart takes flight,
In dances wild beneath the night.

Each whisper tells a story lost,
Of daring hearts and paths uncrossed.
In every laugh, a tear does blend,
As time reveals what dreams ascend.

Like starlit skies, our visions soar,
Unchained, unbound, we yearn for more.
For every wish upon the breeze,
Brings tales of wonder, hopes to seize.

So let the ballad find its tune,
In moonlit nights and morning's bloom.
For untethered dreams shall always gleam,
A testament to life's wild dream.

The Canvas of Untouched Hearts

In shades of silence, colors bloom,
Each stroke a whisper, devoid of gloom.
A canvas wide, yet untouched still,
Dreams ignite, as passions thrill.

Beneath the surface, stories lie,
Unwritten tales in the sky.
With every heartbeat, brushstrokes dance,
Awakening souls to chance.

As shadows mingle, light unfolds,
Fleeting moments, dreams retold.
In the gallery of what could be,
Hearts create their own decree.

With every shade, a truth reveals,
In vibrant hues, the future heals.
Embrace the canvas, soft and wide,
Together, with love as our guide.

Reflections in a Glassy Mist

A foggy dawn, the world anew,
Mirrored dreams in morning dew.
Whispers float on currents mild,
Nature's breath, awake and wild.

Through glassy mist, reflections see,
Fragments of what used to be.
Silhouettes beneath the haze,
Echoes of forgotten days.

With every glance, the heart ignites,
In the stillness, hidden lights.
In clarity, the past aligns,
Moments laced like ancient vines.

Breath of history, soft and sweet,
In this beauty, memories meet.
In glassy mist, we find our way,
Through the shadows of yesterday.

Ephemeral Connections in Twilight

At twilight's edge, where light meets dark,
Connections spark a fleeting arc.
With whispers soft, the stars align,
In fleeting moments, souls entwine.

A gentle hush, the night descends,
Ephemeral ties that time transcends.
In glances shared, stories bloom,
Unspoken words dispel the gloom.

Fading light, where shadows play,
Every heartbeat holds the sway.
In this hour of dreams unfurled,
We create our own small world.

Hold close the dusk, where hopes arise,
In twilight's veil, the spirit flies.
Though transient, love's light endures,
In every heart, its memory stirs.

The Dance of Unfelt Touch

In shadows cast, a dance begins,
With graceful moves, the silence spins.
Unfelt touches ride the air,
A symphony, yet none are there.

With every sway, the hearts rejoice,
In whispered dreams, we find our voice.
Invisible threads weave through the night,
Guiding souls with gentle might.

As moonlight drapes the empty floor,
Memories linger, yearning for more.
In this ballet of silent grace,
We find our steps in time and space.

Though unmarked, this dance we share,
Lives intertwined in the cool night air.
With every breath and fleeting glance,
We lose ourselves within the dance.

Dancing in the Realm of Nonexistence

In shadows where the whispers glide,
We sway upon the edge of dreams,
Each step a fleeting, soft waltz ride,
Where silence births the quiet beams.

Drifting through an endless void,
Our spirits twirl without a care,
In this space, both lost and toyed,
The echoes shimmer, light as air.

No ground to bind our thoughts so free,
We twine with echoes of the past,
In this dance, we cease to be,
Yet feel the love that ever lasts.

With every turn, the world dissolved,
In nonexistence, we embrace,
A timeless realm where hearts resolved,
To find their rest in fleeting grace.

Echo Chamber of Imagined Affections

In chambers where our thoughts collide,
The voices bounce in muted light,
Reflections of the love we bide,
Resounding softly, day and night.

Each whispered promise grips the air,
Yet echoes tremble, twist, and fly,
In intimacy, we lay bare,
But hollow sounds are only sighs.

We craft our dreams with careful art,
Constructing bridges built on trust,
Yet silent truths can tear apart,
The fragile beams we deem as just.

In chambers where our secrets dwell,
Our feelings flutter, twist, and churn,
We yearn for truths we cannot tell,
In echo's grasp, we feel the burn.

Sparks that Never Caught Fire

A flicker in the fading night,
Unkindled flames that held their breath,
In moments lost, we chase the light,
Yet find it stilled by quiet death.

We spark the dreams with hopeful ache,
But winds of doubt snuff every ray,
Each ember found, so prone to break,
A dance of chance that fades away.

In every glance, a promise flares,
But flickers dim before they soar,
With every pulse, the tension pairs,
Yet warmth is lost in memories' war.

These sparks, they swirl in vacant air,
A fleeting glimpse of what could be,
Yet bound by fear, we must beware,
Of fires that led us to be free.

Beauty Found in Theoretical Touch

In concepts where our hearts entwine,
We taste the sweetness, thought so rare,
Imagined warmth, a tender sign,
In theory lost, yet always there.

The gentle brush of fingertips,
A dance of minds that never meet,
In dreams, we share our secret scripts,
Creating worlds beneath our feet.

Each notion blooms in shadows cast,
Where longing echoes, bittersweet,
In fleeting moments, hearts amassed,
Find beauty where our spirits greet.

Though distance shapes what feels so close,
In theory, love can still ascend,
For even in a thought's repose,
We find the touch that won't soon end.

Illusions in the Realm of Togetherness

In shadows cast by whispering dreams,
We walk hand in hand, or so it seems.
A dance of laughter, a fleeting glance,
Bound by illusions, we take our chance.

Yet time unveils the fragile thread,
A tapestry woven with words unsaid.
In the realm where hearts collide,
We search for truth, yet shadows hide.

A tapestry spun with fleeting light,
Promises glimmer, then fade from sight.
Together we stand on this fragile shore,
Yet deep in the night, we're longing for more.

In echoes lost, our whispers wane,
Dancing on air, like ghosts in the rain.
Together we dream, yet drift apart,
An illusion held within a tender heart.

The Anatomy of Afictional Bonds

In the weave of words, we find our place,
A fictional bond, a tender embrace.
Limited touches, infinite ways,
Love penned in silence, brightening days.

Charting the course of unfathomed seas,
We scribble our story like leaves in the breeze.
Yet in the margins, reality bites,
Fiction can falter in the midst of fights.

Mapping emotions through layers of time,
Threads of affection that subtly rhyme.
We draw on the canvas of aching hearts,
With every brushstroke, our world departs.

Yet in this creation, where dreams align,
We seek for meaning in what we define.
Afictional whispers, lost in the night,
Binding our souls with ethereal light.

Between What Is and What Might Be

Caught in the web of what could arise,
The space between dreams and solemn goodbyes.
Questions linger in the twilight hue,
What is and might be, forever askew.

With hearts held high, we chase the stars,
Yet shadows follow, with hidden scars.
In moments rare, choices conspire,
To bridge the chasm, igniting desire.

The path unfolds under fickle skies,
Between the laughter and silent sighs.
Eager to leap, yet fearful to fall,
We balance our hopes against reason's call.

In this delicate dance of fate's decree,
We ponder the gap, what can never be.
An echo of dreams, both tender and free,
Dwells beautifully still, between you and me.

Sketches of Unwritten Love Stories

On pages blank, our hearts reside,
Sketching love tales that merge and glide.
With every heartbeat, a tale untold,
In whispers shared, our lives unfold.

With pencil strokes of passion and fear,
We draw between lines, making it clear.
Each moment captured, a chance to create,
The stories unwritten, entwined by fate.

Silhouettes dance in the soft twilight,
Between dreams of day and serenades of night.
In the margins linger those who will see,
The sketches we hide, from you and from me.

Yet, ink may fade, and paper may fray,
But the love in our hearts will never stray.
For in every glance, every sigh we impart,
Lies the essence of our unwritten art.

The Fragile Architecture of Closure

In the silence, whispers fade,
Promises carved, then unmade.
Windows shut with heavy sighs,
Brick by brick, the walls arise.

Memories linger in the air,
Fractured dreams laid bare.
Mortar mixed with hopes and fears,
Each stone echoes countless years.

Yet through the cracks, light may peep,
A fragile promise we can keep.
For even ruins hold a grace,
In the heart of their embrace.

So let us build with gentle hands,
A structure in shifting sands.
In the end, we'll find a way,
To find closure, come what may.

Spheres of Influence on the Edge of Want

In shadows cast by distant stars,
We dance beneath our dreams of cars.
Whispers bend the lines of fate,
Longing stirs, yet we await.

Circles drawn in fading light,
Colors blend with every night.
Desires pulse, a silent song,
In our hearts, where we belong.

Wants are tangled like the vines,
Time, a thief, of hidden signs.
Yet in the depths of restless thought,
Lies the love we always sought.

So let the spheres collide and spin,
In this dance, we lose and win.
For on the edge, we find the way,
To cherish night, embrace the day.

Traces of Unfulfilled Ambitions

On paper, dreams once brightly soared,
A canvas blank, a mind implored.
Chasing visions, fast and free,
Now shadows whisper, 'What could be?'

Footprints left on roads untried,
Paths forsaken, hopes denied.
Yet glimmers of past aspirations,
Spark like distant constellations.

Time marched on, a ruthless friend,
Woven threads that fray and bend.
But still we reach with weary hands,
To trace the lines of our own plans.

Though unfulfilled, ambitions gleam,
In twilight's hush, we dare to dream.
For every trace, a tale unfolds,
Of courage held, of hearts that bold.

The Hideaway of Could-Be Love

In the corners of our minds,
Lies a place where hope unwinds.
Softly spoken, secrets kept,
In shadows where our hearts have slept.

Dreams of touch, a fleeting glance,
Silent threads in a hesitant dance.
Time will weave what fate may sever,
In this hideaway, we gather.

Whispers linger like morning mist,
In every pause, a chance to kiss.
Yet still we hold the door ajar,
For love awaits, just near and far.

So in this space, we'll learn to find,
The courage buried deep in kind.
For in our hearts, we'll dare to soar,
In the hideaway, forevermore.

Labyrinths of What-Could-Have-Been

Lost in the winding ways,
Memories whisper softly,
Time's tangled threads we trace,
In shadows of dreams, we see.

Paths we never chose to walk,
Echoes of laughter linger,
Forgotten words left unspoken,
In silence, we're left to ponder.

Shoulders brush in fleeting sighs,
Moments woven in the air,
Fates collide with unspent love,
Reveries too deep to bear.

Yet still we roam this maze,
Chasing visions never born,
Through corridors of longing,
'Neath the weight of endless morn.

The Palette of Unsung Melodies

Soft whispers of twilight hues,
Brushstrokes of a fading sun,
Each note a memory unbroken,
In harmony, we come undone.

Colors dance in quiet tongue,
Songs sung by the leaves at night,
A canvas painted with our dreams,
Awakening the stars' delight.

In every chord, an echo glows,
A serenade of hopes set free,
The richness found in silence,
The colors of what's meant to be.

Let us hum these tales of old,
With brush and heart, we shape the air,
A symphony of whispered joys,
In every breath, we lay it bare.

Landscapes of Longed-For Touch

In twilight's gentle embrace,
Fingers brush against the night,
The yearning for a soft caress,
In dreams, we seek the light.

Silhouettes of fleeting hearts,
Craving warmth in shadows cast,
The distance aches, yet still we yearn,
For moments that curl like the past.

Tender whispers through the air,
Crystals of the moon alight,
We reach across the velvet dark,
Finding solace in the night.

Each breath a testament of hope,
A promise in the space between,
In landscapes where our fantasies,
Reveal the love that could have been.

Futile Dances of Sunlit Desires

In garden blooms of bright allure,
We dance in circles made of light,
But petals fall, time whispers low,
Fleeting dreams lost to the night.

Sunlit paths we wander blind,
Chasing beams that slip away,
With every step, we reach for dreams,
And yet, they falter, fade to gray.

Softly swaying with the breeze,
Our laughter turns to distant sighs,
For in the warmth of day we strive,
Only to lose the sun's sweet prize.

Still in this dance, we choose to stay,
Hoping for a chance to find,
That even in the twilight's call,
Desire's fire will not be blind.

Promises in the Air

Whispers dance like leaves in wind,
Dreams entwined, where hopes begin.
Silent vows in twilight's hue,
They echo softly, pure and true.

Stars align in midnight's glow,
Casting shadows on paths we know.
Hearts embrace the gentle light,
As promises gleam, warm and bright.

Through storms that threaten to divide,
A bond unbroken, side by side.
Every heartbeat sings a song,
In this moment, we belong.

In the dawn, our spirits soar,
With every promise, we explore.
Together, we shall always dare,
To weave our dreams, suspended air.

Surreal Emotions Unfold

In shadows cast by fading sun,
Colors blend, a race begun.
Feelings swirl like clouds above,
Mysteries wrapped in layers of love.

Time bends softly in the night,
Reflecting dreams in silver light.
Tangled thoughts, they weave and wane,
Avoiding reason, embracing pain.

Each heartbeat whispers tales untold,
As surreal visions brightly unfold.
Clarity dances in the haze,
Guiding souls through twisted maze.

Emotions flicker, shadows flit,
In this realm where moments sit.
We explore the depths of mind,
In the surreal, truth we find.

The Landscape of Untouched Love

Endless fields of emerald green,
Where whispers linger, love unseen.
Mountains rise, a watchful gaze,
Guarding hearts in quiet praise.

Rivers flow with stories shared,
In every ripple, love declared.
Softest breezes kiss the skies,
Carrying dreams where silence lies.

In the twilight, shadows blend,
A landscape vast, where souls ascend.
Each moment blooms, a fragrant sigh,
In untouched love, we learn to fly.

Stars twinkle in the velvet night,
Guiding us with gentle light.
In this realm where we can roam,
Untouched love, forever home.

Floating in Between

Drifting softly, lost in thought,
In the stillness, solace sought.
Between the worlds of night and day,
We find the dreams that lead the way.

A tender sigh, a fleeting glance,
In this space, we dare to dance.
Time suspended, moments blend,
Floating softly without end.

Waves of hope, they crash and pull,
In the silence, hearts are full.
Caught between the now and then,
We gather strength to start again.

In the twilight where shadows meet,
We embrace all that feels complete.
Floating in between we find,
A woven thread, forever twined.

Musings of a Heart Unknown

In shadows deep, where silence sighs,
A heart beats softly, lost in lies.
Whispers dance in twilight's glow,
Secrets held where few would go.

Each moment drifts like autumn leaves,
Time weaves patterns, hope believes.
Yet in the stillness, longing grows,
An echo of what nobody knows.

In dreams I wander, paths unknown,
Through fields of thought, seeds are sown.
What truths lie hidden, what tales untold?
In this heart's chamber, love unfolds.

So here I stand, with fears unveiled,
A tapestry of wishes, frail.
In quiet ruminations, I find my way,
To the essence of love, come what may.

Reveries of the Unseen

Beneath the veil, a world resides,
Where mystery and magic abides.
In whispered dreams, we find our place,
Eclipsed by time, in endless grace.

Each fleeting glance, a story spun,
Moments lurking, never done.
In shadows cast by moon's embrace,
Life's secrets dwell in fleeting space.

A silent flicker, a gentle sigh,
Echoes linger, the reason why.
In the silence, visions gleam,
Through the unseen, we chase our dream.

Yet through the darkness, hope will rise,
A flickering flame that never dies.
In reveries woven from heart and mind,
The unseen paths, our souls will find.

Unwritten Affection

A glance that lingers, words unsaid,
In the quiet linger, emotions tread.
Hearts entwined in unspoken ways,
Finding solace in the gentle gaze.

Invisible threads that softly weave,
Stories of love we dare believe.
Each heartbeat whispers secrets rare,
In the silence, we lay our care.

A touch that sparks a silent fire,
In the depth of longing, we aspire.
Unwritten pages, in shadows cast,
Moments cherished, though they pass.

In every sigh, our spirits sing,
Promises bloom in the hope they bring.
An unwritten tale, an endless quest,
In the warmth of affection, we find our rest.

Gems of Nature's Dreams

In the dawn's light, petals unfold,
Stories of nature, timeless and bold.
Each dewdrop glistens, a fleeting grace,
Nature's jewels in this sacred place.

Mountains whisper, rivers hum,
In windswept skies, the heartbeats drum.
Every rustle tells tales of old,
Gems of life in colors untold.

From valleys deep to oceans wide,
In nature's arms, we take our stride.
A canvas painted with vibrant hue,
Reflecting dreams of a world anew.

With every sunset, a promise made,
In the twilight's glow, our worries fade.
Gems of nature's heart, forever gleam,
As we wander through life's gentle dream.

The Fabric of Fabled Affections

In twilight's glow, we weave our dreams,
Threads of laughter, gentle beams.
Fables dance in shadows deep,
Promises in silence keep.

Metaphors crafted with tender care,
Stories linger in the air.
Hearts entwined, a tapestry spun,
Forever bound, two become one.

Through starlit nights, our visions soar,
Echoes of love through every door.
We stitch the moments, bright and rare,
In the fabric of fabled affairs.

With every stitch, the memories grow,
In every thread, our spirits glow.
A lasting bond that we create,
In this world of shared fate.

Dreamscapes of Yearning

In dream's embrace, we find our space,
Where echoes of longing leave their trace.
Wandering pathways of our mind,
In the depths, what will we find?

Whispers linger, sweet and low,
Through the shadows, passions flow.
In twilight realms, our hopes ignite,
Chasing stars through endless night.

A canvas painted with desire,
In the silence, hearts conspire.
Every heartbeat, a silent plea,
In these dreamscapes, you and me.

Awakening to the tender call,
Yearning echoes, never small.
For in each dream, our spirits dance,
In the realm of love's romance.

Whispers of Unrealized Amours

In quiet moments, secrets sigh,
Unrealized dreams that flutter by.
Hearts unspoken, words unsaid,
In this silence, love is bred.

Fleeting glances, a tender flinch,
Lost opportunities make us wince.
In the shadows, feelings bloom,
In the dark, we find our room.

A longing glance, it lingers still,
What could be, if hearts would spill?
Whispers linger, soft and sweet,
In unrealized love, we meet.

Through the echoes, fate aligns,
In every pause, a chance defines.
Yet we cherish what might have been,
In the whispers, love's unseen.

Imaginary Collisions of Souls

Two worlds collide in unseen grace,
Imaginary realms we dare to trace.
In the spark of a fleeting glance,
Souls entwined in a silent dance.

With every touch, the cosmos gleams,
In our fantasies, boundless dreams.
In this realm where time stands still,
Hearts collide with sheer will.

In cosmic tides, our feelings soar,
A collision of spirits, evermore.
In whispered secrets that we share,
A universe blooms in the air.

As stardust lingers in our wake,
Infinite paths that fate will make.
Connected souls across the night,
Imaginary worlds bathed in light.

The Soul's Elusive Debris

In whispers soft, the echoes play,
Fragments of dreams drift far away.
Shadows murmur, secrets weave,
In silence deep, we dare believe.

A tapestry of hopes and fears,
Woven tight with laughter, tears.
The weight of past, light as a sigh,
Scattered hints beneath the sky.

Yet in the dark, a spark ignites,
Guiding hearts through lonely nights.
With every breath, the truth unfolds,
Instincts ancient, stories told.

Through fleeting moments, we embrace,
The soul's debris, a sacred space.
An odyssey of all we've known,
In every shard, a light is shown.

Reflections in the Realm of Possibility

Mirrors glint with hidden dreams,
Endless paths and shining streams.
Each choice a bloom in twilight's grace,
In dawn's embrace, we find our place.

Infinite whispers guide the way,
In silent hopes, we long to stay.
The heart knows where it needs to roam,
In this realm, we craft our home.

Stars align with every breath,
Defining life, defying death.
In every glance, a chance to see,
The beauty of our destiny.

In the dance of fate, we learn,
With every twist, the fires burn.
Reflections bright, the world in view,
In possibility, all things are true.

Fleeting Phantoms of Desire

Whispers linger in moonlit nights,
Fleeting dreams take fragile flights.
Echoes chase the waking hours,
As hope blooms like fleeting flowers.

In velvet shadows, secrets sigh,
Yearning hearts that never die.
With every touch, a promise fades,
In fleeting moments, love parades.

A dance of shadows, lost and found,
In silence deep, our souls resound.
The pulse of night, a haunting thrill,
Fleeting phantoms, hearts to fill.

Yet as dawn breaks, dreams take flight,
Chasing phantoms into light.
In the quiet, we hold the fire,
As life unfolds, our sweet desire.

Chimeras of Love's Echo

In whispers soft, love's echoes swell,
Chimeras cast a fragrant spell.
In twilight's glow, the heart will chase,
The tender lines of each embrace.

Mirages dance in starlit air,
Brief as time, yet always there.
Each glance a thread that intertwines,
In woven dreams, our fate defines.

The music plays, a sweet refrain,
Through joy and loss, through grief and gain.
In every heartbeat, love's refrain,
Chimeras of joy, rise again.

Time slips by, yet memories stay,
In every laugh, a soft bouquet.
Through light and dark, the echoes roam,
In love's embrace, we've found our home.

Fabricating Love's Echo

In whispers soft, we weave our dreams,
With threads of hope, love's gentle seams.
Each vow a spark, ignites the night,
Together we dance in pure delight.

In the quiet dusk, our hearts align,
Creating echoes, sweet and divine.
In every glance, a story unfolds,
A tapestry rich, with hues of gold.

Shadows of What Could Be

In twilight's grasp, our shadows merge,
With silent tales, our spirits surge.
A longing glance, a fleeting sigh,
In dreams we soar, yet never fly.

The moments passed, like ghosts they roam,
In paths untread, we find our home.
Yet hope remains, a flickering flame,
In shadows deep, we play love's game.

Romantic Daydreams Unbound

Beneath the stars, our thoughts take flight,
In daydreams bright, we chase the light.
A soft caress, a longing smile,
Together we wander, mile by mile.

With every heartbeat, a spark ignites,
In the hush of dusk, our love ignites.
Through whispered words, our souls entwined,
In romantic realms, true love we find.

Illusions of Tenderness

In fleeting moments, our hearts may blend,
With gentle caress, love has no end.
Yet in the shadows, doubts may rise,
Illusions fade beneath the skies.

A tender touch, a fragile thread,
In longing dreams, where silence led.
But somewhere deep, our truth remains,
In whispers soft, love breaks the chains.

The Breath of Fleeting Certainty

In whispers soft, the moments flee,
A sigh that dances, wild and free.
The light of dawn, it flickers low,
Yet in its glow, our hopes will grow.

Each truth we chase, it shifts away,
Like shadows cast at end of day.
Yet still we reach with trembling hands,
For certainty on shifting sands.

A touch, a glance, a fleeting smile,
We gather dreams and run awhile.
The breath of life, a fragile song,
In every note, we still belong.

And when it fades, like morning mist,
We'll hold the echoes, can't resist.
For in the heart, though doubts may stay,
The breath of certainty leads the way.

Heartstrings of Approached but Untouched

In shadows cast, our eyes collide,
A language spoken deep inside.
With breath held close, the silence sings,
Of heartstrings pulled, but not of things.

The moments linger, sweet and shy,
In glances brief, we dare to fly.
Yet every step feels out of reach,
For love lies close, but fears still preach.

A tender glance, a fleeting touch,
In dreams we find, we long so much.
But fears arise and hearts retreat,
As longing swells, we know defeat.

Yet in the dark, our wishes glow,
With every beat, our secrets flow.
In silence held, we dare to trust,
For heartstrings bind where love is just.

An Opera of Unheard Notes

The stage is set, the curtains drawn,
In silence deep, the night is born.
A symphony of dreams untold,
In every heart, a story bold.

The music swells, though none can hear,
In whispered winds, the notes appear.
Each longing pulse, a silent plea,
An opera of what's meant to be.

With every breath, a chance we take,
To dance along, to dream, awake.
The melodies of hope arise,
In secret glances, hidden sighs.

Though time may weave a tangled thread,
The song of life is never dead.
In every heart, we find our role,
An opera that ignites the soul.

The Unsaid Words Between Two Stars

In the vast night, two stars collide,
With silent wishes, side by side.
Their light entwined, a cosmic dance,
In whispered hopes, they take their chance.

Unseen by eyes, the stories weave,
Of dreams unspoken, hearts that grieve.
Yet in the dark, their spirits soar,
In every spark, they seek for more.

The weight of things they dare not say,
A universe in disarray.
For in their light, a truth abides,
The unsaid words that love divides.

But in the silence, strength will grow,
Across the sky, their bodies flow.
And though apart, their hearts will glow,
Together strong in night's tableau.

Imagined Affections

In shadows where soft whispers play,
Emotions dance, they find their way.
Hearts entwined, though worlds apart,
A silent song, a hidden art.

Wistful gazes in the night,
Thoughts alight, a fleeting flight.
In dreams we share, our spirits soar,
Imagined views that ask for more.

Fingers trace the air so light,
Catching feelings, pure delight.
In secret realms, our wishes blend,
Unspoken truths that never end.

These tender ties, like fragile threads,
We weave anew where hope spreads.
In dreams of us, the heart's embrace,
Imagined affections fill the space.

Dreams of Unseen Bonds

Across the stars, our spirits meet,
In whispered thoughts, a love so sweet.
Invisible ties hold us near,
A connection forged beyond all fear.

In twilight's glow, we find our thread,
Voices soft where others tread.
In silent nights, our wishes bloom,
Dreams of bonds that chase the gloom.

Through misty paths, we wander free,
In realms of light, just you and me.
Each heartbeat sings a secret song,
In dreams, my love, where we belong.

Our hearts unite like hidden springs,
In unseen realms, where magic clings.
With every dream, our worlds converge,
Unseen bonds, a gentle urge.

Whispers in the Void

In silence deep, the echoes call,
Whispers rise, and shadows fall.
A canvas vast, the stars align,
In cosmic dance, our dreams entwine.

Through endless night, our hopes confide,
In starlit realms, where we can glide.
Each secret murmur, soft and low,
Carries warmth in the dark below.

In voids profound, our voices blend,
In softest tones that never end.
A lullaby for souls adrift,
Whispers guide each subtle shift.

With every breath, the silence sings,
In hidden depths, a universe springs.
Together we float, lost in the sound,
In whispers of love, forever bound.

Fantasies of the Unspoken

In twilight's hush, thoughts intertwine,
Fantasies bloom, so sweet, divine.
Words unvoiced, yet deeply felt,
In silent dreams, our hearts have dwelt.

With tender glances, secrets shared,
In uncharted realms, we are ensnared.
Gentle strokes of fate align,
In fantasies that brightly shine.

In every sigh, a promise waits,
With yearning eyes, we contemplate.
Unspoken bonds that linger long,
In shadows cast, our souls grow strong.

Across the dark, where silence reigns,
We find our peace amidst the chains.
In dreams we weave, a tapestry,
Fantasies of love, wild and free.

Mirages in the Garden of Romance

Beneath the blooms where shadows dance,
Whispers linger, lost in chance.
Petals fall like secrets shared,
In a world where hearts are bared.

Graceful vines entwine with ease,
Promises float upon the breeze.
Time stands still in this serene,
Where love's light and hope convene.

Yet the sun begins to wane,
Painting dreams with soft disdain.
Mirages fade as night descends,
The garden sleeps, as daylight ends.

Fragments of a Collapsed Daydream

In the corners of my mind,
Fractured pieces intertwined.
What once shone now dims away,
Hope's reflection in dismay.

Clouds gather, casting doubt,
Silent screams begin to shout.
The dreamscape crumbles, dust to dust,
All that lingered fades to rust.

Yet amidst this tangled mess,
Glimmers of unwitnessed bliss.
Though shattered, I still try to see,
A glimpse of what could never be.

The Paradox of Phantom Passions

In twilight's grasp, hearts intertwine,
Fleeting dreams, a trace divine.
Burning bright, yet never near,
A love that whispers, unclear.

Shadows dance where silence reigns,
Echoes trapped in love's refrain.
The heart knows well what it cannot have,
A bittersweet lie it learns to salve.

Endless cycles of hope and woe,
Yearning for what might never grow.
Still the phantom stays entwined,
In the labyrinth of the mind.

Threads of a Shattered Reverie

Silken strings of memory fray,
Tangled webs where dreams decay.
In the quiet, silence cries,
Lost in the depth of faded skies.

Moments weave through time's embrace,
Each a fragment, a lost trace.
Images broken, scattered light,
Fading swiftly into night.

Yet within this broken weave,
Lies a whisper that won't leave.
In every tear, a story told,
In the dark, the heart turns bold.

Reveries in the Land of Maybe

In the land where dreams take flight,
Whispers dance in soft moonlight.
Hope and doubt entwined in play,
Chasing shadows, they drift away.

Each thought a feather, light and free,
Drifting on winds of mystery.
Time's embrace, a gentle sigh,
In this realm, we learn to fly.

Horizons blur, reality bends,
Every journey has no end.
Softly spoken, the secrets fade,
In the land where dreams are made.

With open hearts, we share the night,
Beneath the stars, all feels right.
In every whisper, every hum,
The land of maybe has begun.

Reflections Upon the Edge of Forever

At the cusp of time's grand sweep,
Where lost moments gently weep.
Stars align in tales untold,
Shimmering dreams of silver and gold.

Rippling waves of endless sea,
Echo with what's yet to be.
Each heartbeat, a timeless song,
Carried forth where we belong.

In whispered winds, the past resides,
Guiding souls as time divides.
With every glance, we touch the light,
Reflections cradle day and night.

On the edge where shadows fade,
In the silence, promises made.
A glimpse of what we hope to find,
In forever's grace, intertwined.

Echoes of Possibilities Unseen

Beneath the surface, whispers stir,
A world of chance, like distant blur.
Each echo holds a tale untold,
Of paths not taken, dreams of bold.

Looming choices dance before,
In the silence, potential's roar.
Eyes closed tight, yet still we see,
The golden thread of destiny.

In every heartbeat, futures twine,
Glimmers of what may be mine.
Step by step, the world unfolds,
In echoes soft, the truth is told.

What lies ahead, we cannot know,
Yet hope will bloom, and stories grow.
In dreams we weave our fate anew,
Echoes sing of what is true.

The Atrium of Unshared Hearts

In shadows cast where silence reigns,
Unseen burdens, unvoiced pains.
The atrium holds the weight of dreams,
Where longing flickers, softly gleams.

Two souls wander, paths apart,
In the chambers of the heart.
Echoes linger, barely felt,
In the space where love can melt.

Eyes connect, but words remain,
Wrapped in layers of quiet pain.
A fleeting glance, a breathless sigh,
In the atrium where hopes lie.

Yet from the stillness, courage grows,
In whispered winds, affection flows.
With every breath, a chance to start,
In the atrium of unshared hearts.

Fleeting Whispers on the Wind

Softly they drift, like leaves in the air,
Carrying secrets, without a care.
Whispers of dreams, they weave and they glide,
Echoes of thoughts that time cannot hide.

Rippling through trees, they paint the day,
Moments forgotten, yet still find their way.
In the hush of dusk, they linger awhile,
Inviting the heart to pause and to smile.

A sigh softly dances on gossamer threads,
Tracing the journey where memory treads.
Caught in the twilight, they flicker and fade,
Leaving us wondering, the price that we paid.

For in quiet whispers, we find our own song,
In the fleeting moments, where we feel we belong.
Hold tight the echoes, let them not fade,
In every soft whisper, our love is displayed.

The Weight of an Untraveled Path

Beneath the trees, the shadows grow long,
A dusty road where footsteps belong.
But onward we stand, with choices unmade,
Guided by dreams that are starting to wade.

Each step not taken, a burden to bear,
The weight of the future hangs heavy in air.
Moments unchosen, like leaves on the ground,
Whispers of paths where our hopes can be found.

Winding through forests, in silence we pause,
Reflecting on what lies beneath our own flaws.
The call of the wild, both fierce and serene,
Awakens the heart to what might have been.

Yet still, we wander, for journeys await,
In the dance with the unknown, we seize our fate.
With courage ignited, we soften our stance,
Embracing the mystery of life's fleeting chance.

The Silence After the Hypothetical Kiss

In a breath held tight, the world holds its breath,
Moments suspended, between life and death.
A question unasked, a longing in view,
As silence envelops, it whispers of you.

Time seems to pause, like the calm before rain,
A pulse in the still, it pulses through pain.
Every heartbeat echoes, a gentle refrain,
In the unspoken, love dances with gain.

Will we ever know, what the touch could ignite?
In the hush of goodbye, dreams shimmer with light.
For silence can speak, louder than sound,
In the space between us, what magic is found?

Yet memories linger, in twilight's embrace,
Holding the sweetness of dreams we can't chase.
Some moments remain, shrouded in mist,
Forever they echo, the kiss that we missed.

Colors of a Nonexistent Flame

In the dark of night, colors take flight,
Imagined hues that defy the light.
Whispers of crimson, and sapphire skies,
Every shade trembles, where silence lies.

Flames that don't flicker, but pulse in our mind,
The warmth of a fire, forever entwined.
Brush strokes of longing in shades of despair,
Painting the night with dreams of the rare.

In a void without color, a spark still remains,
Vibrant and subtle, like soft summer rains.
Each heartbeat a canvas, our souls intertwine,
Crafting a world where the spirits align.

Though nothing may burn, and shadows may fade,
The essence of color will never evade.
In the depths of our hearts, a glow we reclaim,
Forever ignited, a non-existent flame.

Phantoms of Togetherness

In shadows cast by fading light,
Whispers dance in the cool of night.
Echoes linger, hearts entwined,
A memory built, a love defined.

Through silent whispers, dreams we braid,
In twilight's glow, our fears allayed.
Together we walk, though paths divide,
In the phantoms, our hearts reside.

Time may wane, yet bonds remain,
Through joy and sorrow, love's refrain.
In spectral forms, we find our way,
Forever held, though worlds decay.

With every pulse, a thread we weave,
In the realm of the heart, we believe.
Though distance may play its fateful game,
The phantoms return, love's eternal flame.

Flights of Fancy in Love

On wings of dreams, we dare to soar,
To heights where silence sings once more.
With hearts unbound, we chase the stars,
In fantasy's realm, love knows no bars.

Through gardens lush, our laughter weaves,
In vibrant hues, a tapestry believes.
With every glance, a universe spun,
In flights of fancy, two become one.

In gentle breezes, our secrets shared,
In moonlit nights, we dream unprepared.
With whispers soft, our spirits rise,
In love's embrace, we touch the skies.

With every heartbeat, a promise laid,
In the dance of dreams, we won't be swayed.
Together we soar, hand in hand,
In flights of fancy, love's magic planned.

Veils of Desire

In shadows cast, a mystery lies,
With longing glances and secret sighs.
Beneath the veils, desires ignite,
In whispered breaths, we chase the night.

With every touch, a spark unfolds,
In silent pleas, our truth behold.
Through winding paths of passion's call,
In the veils of desire, we rise and fall.

In heartbeats quick, a dance in time,
With tangled limbs, our souls align.
Through fervent flames, we taste the fire,
In the glow of love, unfiltered by desire.

As morning breaks, the veils dissolve,
In tender light, we find resolve.
With every shadow now left behind,
We walk as one, in love's design.

A Tapestry of Longing

Threads of color in time's embrace,
We weave our dreams, a sacred space.
With every stitch, a story told,
In the tapestry of longing, we find our gold.

Moments captured like stars that shine,
In the fabric of love, your hand in mine.
Through storms and calm, our hearts align,
In threads of hope, our spirits intertwine.

With every heartbeat, we weave anew,
Colors merging, shades of you.
In the loom of life, we craft our fate,
In a tapestry of longing, we create.

As twilight falls, our work laid bare,
In every fold, love's gentle care.
With threads of memories spun so bright,
In our tapestry, we find the light.

Imagined Embraces at Dusk

In twilight's gentle glow so bright,
Whispers of dreams take flight,
Soft shadows dance with the night,
Yearning hearts feel the light.

The stars unfold their timeless grace,
In solitude, I seek your face,
Fingers brush in this empty space,
In imagined embraces, we trace.

Moonlight casts a silver seam,
As night drapes over the dream,
In every sigh, a silent scream,
Holding on to love's lost theme.

Lost in thoughts where warmth resides,
Time melts like the ebbing tides,
In the silence, hope abides,
Imagined embraces, love provides.

Specters of Longing in the Breeze

Through whispering leaves, I feel you near,
Ghostly echoes that disappear,
Fleeting moments drawn so clear,
Specters of longing, ever dear.

The wind carries soft, sweet sighs,
Memories linger, never dies,
Thoughts entwined in starry skies,
In each breath, love softly lies.

Your laughter lingers in the air,
Remnants of you, everywhere,
In shadows, I sense you dare,
To haunt my heart with tender care.

With each turn, these visions tease,
In the twilight, I find my ease,
Longing whispers on the breeze,
Specters command the heart to seize.

Tales of Unsaid Promises

Within the silence, words remain,
Fragments of wishes, ghostly pain,
Promises lost, yet not in vain,
In twilight's hush, I call your name.

Woven in the fabric of trust,
In the stillness, rise the must,
These unspoken thoughts, so robust,
Longing to bloom, like stardust.

Beneath the sky's vast, aching dome,
Where shadows whisper, and dreams roam,
I search for the path that leads home,
To tales of promises, not alone.

Time bends slowly, a tender thread,
In the echoes of all that's said,
Sip from the chalice of love, widespread,
In the courage of words, unled.

Ghosts of Hearts Not Yet Met

In the quiet moments before the dawn,
Where dreams linger, though they're gone,
Ghosts of hearts await the morn,
With every breath, the world is drawn.

Fingers brushing against fate's skin,
In shadows where the light begins,
A future waits, like whispered sins,
For connections deep, where love spins.

Each heartbeat echoes, soft and shy,
In the distance, a soft goodbye,
Yet through the dusk, we still reply,
To ghosts of hearts, we can't deny.

With every sunset, new hopes emerge,
As lives entwine in love's large surge,
In the silence, our spirits urge,
To find each other, and then converge.

Shadows of Unchased Dreams

In the silent corners of my mind,
Shadows dance with whispers kind.
They weave through moments, lost and fleet,
Chasing echoes of dreams, bittersweet.

Fleeting glances, like morning dew,
Fading fast, yet always true.
A montage of hopes that never soared,
Trapped in time, forever ignored.

Ghostly visions under moonlit skies,
A canvas painted with silent sighs.
Each stroke a story that time won't keep,
In shadows of dreams, where sorrows seep.

Yet from the darkness, a light may beam,
Rekindling the flicker of a brave dream.
In the heart's hidden chambers, we find,
A softness to which the soul is blind.

Holograms in the Theatre of Affection

In the dim-lit room where feelings blend,
Holograms shimmer, their forms transcend.
Dancing lightly through strangers' sights,
In the theatre of love, we chase the lights.

Softened voices twine in the air,
Promises linger, a delicate snare.
Yet shadows creep with silent grace,
Unraveling dreams in this fragile space.

The laughter echoes in rooms they left,
Pieces of self, a broken theft.
Yet amidst the chaos, hearts still yearn,
For warmth and connection, a lesson learned.

With each curtain fall, the silence grows,
An empty stage where affection flows.
In holograms' glow, we find our way,
Back to moments where love would stay.

Odysseys of the Unborn Yearn

In the twilight, futures spin,
Where whispers of wonder gently begin.
Odysseys forged in silence and clay,
Yearning for dawn to light the way.

Unseen journeys, paths yet to tread,
Hopes intertwined in dreams we shed.
Carried on winds of what may come,
Echoes of laughter, the unborn hum.

Beneath the surface, our spirits soar,
Charting the skies for the dreams we wore.
With every heartbeat, a story unfolds,
Of love's sweet promise, yet to be told.

In the womb of time, futures will grow,
The seeds of tomorrow, softly aglow.
With each silent wish, we give them flight,
Seeking the day from the depths of night.

The Quiet Afterthoughts of Love

In the aftermath of whispered vows,
Quiet thoughts linger, gentle brows.
Memories dance in soft retreads,
Filling the spaces where silence spreads.

Time stretches slowly, like a breath,
In the stillness, we ponder depth.
The echoes of laughter, the sighs unspoken,
Fragments of hearts, both tender and broken.

Amidst the quiet, a warmth remains,
Comfort found in the soft refrains.
Where every glance speaks of what's missed,
In the hush of love, we quietly exist.

These afterthoughts cradle the heart,
A gentle reminder, never apart.
In silence, we find what words can't tell,
The quiet afterthoughts of love's sweet spell.

Milton Keynes UK
Ingram Content Group UK Ltd.
UKHW022116251124
451529UK00012B/553